Let's Manifest Miracles
and Clardy Malugen

"After utilizing the Law of Attraction for years and then working with Rhonda Byrne to launch *The Secret*, we were well versed on the keys to manifesting. Then we were exposed to Clardy Malugen's wonderful book, *Let's Manifest Miracles!* and experienced a number of revelations. There is something uniquely special about Clardy's work. She has a way of expressing things in such a powerfully simple way, you just can't help but get engaged, and track the newer, bigger dreams you were born to have. We highly recommend that you grab a copy and remind yourself of your own passion and power. You'll find yourself quickly manifesting miracles all around you—just like the ones we continue to experience daily." *John & Katie Stellar,* **Stellar Communications,** *e-pr.com, Los Angeles, CA*

"Wow! *Let's Manifest Miracles!* is a great read. I love Clardy Malugen's writing style—you feel like she is right there coaching you. In addition to being a clear and practical guide, the book has a power that reaches out to the reader with blasts of clarity. I had a couple of epiphanies that stopped me in my tracks! The book also rehabilitated several dreams I had abandoned which has completely revitalized my life. I highly recommend this book as a way to experience Clardy Malugen's work—and reconnect with your dreams!"
Mary Yeager, Financial Services, New York, NY

"Clardy Malugen has manifested miracles her whole life. Since we were colleagues in Los Angeles, I have seen and experienced her remarkable gift of touching the lives of those around her and have watched the dramatic results that seem to occur. It just comes naturally for her. Now her book, *Let's Manifest Miracles!*, shares her story and her processes to help the entire planet heal one person at a time. The easy-to-follow guidance and the heartwarming stories she shares of her personal experiences will encourage you to take action and immediately manifest your own miracles."
Lance Avery Morgan, author, **The Society Diplomat,** *Austin, Texas*

"We all know it is important to stay positive, set goals, and visualize outcomes, but Clardy Malugen takes this to a higher level. It's is not just the material she is presenting, or the exercises, or her gift for identifying self defeating patterns, that shifts people. I think people are shifted most by getting a feel for her own energy pattern and model of the world. Anyone who would like to jump start their life would do well to plug in to Clardy's work. It is life-changing."

John Tatum, M.D., **Optimal Health & Learning Center**, *Winter Park & New Smyrna Beach, FL*

"I am happy to report dramatic and tangible results from my work with Clardy Malugen. She helped me clearly identify the issues and patterns that were preventing me from achieving success both in my career and my personal life. With a renewed sense of focus, I envisioned and have created a new, fulfilling relationship with a wonderful man; started my own company; and now fully enjoy the time I have with my daughter. I highly recommend her work to anyone who is looking for positive, healthy change. Her holistic approach to viewing your life will quickly set you on the right track."

Alison D. Buzyniski, President, **LivingLegacy Consultancy, LLC**, *Orlando, FL*

"I prayed for a person like Clardy to come into my life. She has shown me that just a mere shift in your thoughts can change everything: that moment, your day, your entire life. I have learned the simple fact that you can choose to be negative or you can choose to be positive in every moment, every situation. It is truly that simple. It has been incredible for me to see myself break old habits, develop new healthy relationships and completely change my train of thought. I have goosebumps thinking about my future. I highly encourage everyone to check-out Clardy and her work. It will change your life—in more ways than you can possibly imagine."

Missi Mitchell, Personal Trainer/Transitions Lifestyle Coach, **Elite Strength and Fitness**, *Winter Park, FL*

LET'S *Manifest* MIRACLES!

Unleash the Amazing Power of Your Thoughts and Energy

Clardy Malugen, MA, MFA

The Prosperity Experiment
Magnificence Project, LLC
PO Box 2929
Winter Park, FL 32790
407-644-8833
prosperityexp.com

Library of Congress Cataloging-in-Publication Data
Malugen, Clardy
Let's Manifest Miracles! / Clardy Malugen.
    p. cm.

ISBN 978-0-9823928-7-4 (tradepaper)
    1. Self-actualization (psychology) 2. New Thought. 3. Success. 1. Title.
                                        2010915231

Printed in the USA.
Cover design by Gregory Cannon
Distributed by The Magnificence Project, LLC

To my two favorite miracles:

Dylan and Jamie

"These babies are such a joy!"

Contents

Introduction

Introduction

The greatest discovery of my generation is
that a human being can alter his life
by altering his attitudes of mind.
William James (1842-1910)

We are living during an amazing time in the history of the planet. There couldn't be a better time to create a new definition of the word "miracle". We are all experiencing an enormous opportunity to step back, evaluate our lives, discover what is truly important to us, and make the changes necessary to bring us back to our natural state: a life of joy, peace, and prosperity. Although some of the challenges facing our society seem insurmountable at times, the truth is that there has never been a time of more hope. That hope lies in the conscious creation of miracles.

As quantum physics intersects with molecular biology and modern spirituality, we can no longer accept the suggestion that miracles are inexplicable, random events that defy the laws of nature. We are now learning that those ancient tales of miracles and divine intervention may not be so inexplicable after all!

I am grateful that millions of people have been introduced to the concept of the Law of Attraction through the popular book and film, The Secret. Although new to many, this concept has been around for centuries. In a nutshell, the Law of Attraction states that you will attract into your life whatever you focus your energy on. Following my years of study in fields such as psychology, behavioral adaptation, hypnotherapy, spirituality, health, fitness, and body-mind health alternatives, I have come to believe that experimenting with the concept of the Law of Attraction can be a simple key to taking control of your life—and ultimately creating a life that is truly miraculous.

I have been experimenting with the Law of Attraction for as long as I can remember. As a highly intuitive child, I was convinced that I had invented it! As an adult, miracles seemed to easily appear every time I stepped out of my hectic schedule and "remembered" the Law of Attraction. But it was not until 1998 that I realized that the path to consciously creating miracles was also the path to quickly identifying and eliminating self-defeating behavior patterns—and ultimately, the path to becoming reacquainted with your infinitely powerful authentic self. When I connected these dots and developed the Prosperity Experiment process, I felt like I had hit the jackpot. Since then, I have shared this important information with private clients and in workshops, seminars, and online classes. I have been amazed at the astounding successes of my students. It quickly became clear to me that experimenting with these concepts can lead to truly remarkable results. I am convinced that there's not a faster, simpler way to discover and let go of whatever is holding you back. And, in the process, you'll find yourself face to face with the miraculous life of your dreams.

The purpose of this book is to start at the beginning—and help you take the idea of the Law of Attraction a few steps further in the simplest way possible. You'll discover the secrets to making truly significant changes in your life. You'll be able to shift your life quickly and effectively. You'll learn to easily manifest any of your desires. New career, new home, new car, unexpected windfall, soulmate, marriage? No problem. Piece of cake. But the biggest payoff comes as you are naturally led to let go of your ego and merge with your own authentic self. That's when truly dramatic results start to occur effortlessly. That's the place of big miracles.

The first step? Becoming aware of your thoughts and your emotions. New research has proven that the repetition of thoughts can actually alter brain chemistry. As you take back control of your thoughts, you will find that you are also able to control the feelings and emotions that create your energy state. How you choose to use your personal energy determines virtually everything about your life, as the Law of Attraction clearly teaches us. Choosing in every moment to use your energy wisely is the key to consciously creating miracles in your life.

This book is designed to be an "energy-shifting experience." It was carefully crafted to be the catalyst for your conscious miracles—miracles that you will create from your energy and your visions. Once you "get it" and apply the simple concepts to your life, you will quickly understand that your own power is infinite, and that miracles not only exist, but are commonplace. It may sound too simple right now, but as you live these concepts, you will easily grasp their truth and power. Your life choices will come into clear focus, as you find yourself intimately experiencing your oneness with the source of all energy. You will naturally move toward your dreams with joy and passion. Your new focus will quickly shift your life—and the lives of those around you.

Sound a little too airy-fairy, new-agey to you? Confused by the word "manifest"? Completely stymied by phrases like "oneness with the source" and "authentic self"? No problem. Many of my business clients never hear those words from me, but the process is the same. We identify their passions, eliminate their negative patterns and habits, create a game plan, and...voilá... miracles happen. Every time.

I assure you that you can easily create occurrences that will seem to completely defy those old laws of science and nature. Your miracles will astonish you, encourage you, and enrich your life in ways you have never imagined. Consciously creating miracles is not only possible, it is happening every day—in my life and in the lives of millions of people who are open to experimenting with these updated laws of science and nature.

I hope you will take the first step and begin now to enjoy the limitless, miraculous life that you were born to live, as we work together to create our ultimate goal: a healthy, sustainable planet that is brimming with the energy of joy, peace, and prosperity.

There are two ways to live:
you can live as if
nothing is a miracle;
you can live as if
everything is a miracle.

Albert Einstein

Chapter One

WHAT'S THE DEAL WITH THE LAW OF ATTRACTION?

Five Little Words

Chapter One

WHAT'S THE DEAL WITH THE LAW OF ATTRACTION?

Five Little Words

> Ask, and it shall be given you;
> seek, and ye shall find; knock,
> and it shall be opened unto you.
> *Luke 11:9, King James Bible*

If you are already familiar with the Law of Attraction, you probably know that it isn't complicated.

No matter how many books you read, DVDs you watch, or audios you listen to, it always gets back to the same information. That information can easily be distilled into five simple words:

Ask and you will receive.

We've all heard the phrase "ask and you will receive," as well as its many variations. It is clearly expressed in most spiritual texts. Just pick one, you'll find the concept right there.

What most people just don't get is this: it's true.

Literally.

If you truly desire something and you ask for it clearly, you will receive it. Period. This is not an obtuse metaphor with layers of deep meanings. We're not kidding around here. All you have to do is **ask**.

That's honestly all you have to know. So stop complicating it.

The $2500 Miracle

Several years ago, when I lived in Los Angeles, I was in a transition period between closing one company and opening another. I had decided that it was time to let go of my small rent-controlled apartment and find a more spacious, more nurturing home. I knew that it would be difficult to find a rental in the wonderful neighborhood that I desired, but I also believed that with visualization, anything is possible. I carefully created my vision of the perfect home. Within a couple of weeks, following a series of coincidences, the perfect home "appeared" right on schedule, and I happily moved in. In my negotiations for the lease, I had given the landlord a large sum of money for deposits, rent, and related expenses, which created a temporary cash flow crunch.

On the day of this "miracle," I was sitting at my desk, looking outside at my pool, feeling grateful for my beautiful new home. I had just moved in and had one of those moments of amazement that my vision had indeed created the perfect reality.

As I was sitting there, filled with gratitude, my phone rang. It was the bank. I knew my bankers well, since I had always deposited large sums of money into my accounts when my company was doing well. I had made a large deposit prior to writing the checks for my lease, so I was wondering why they were calling. The news was not good. "Clardy, one of the checks that you deposited last week has been returned. The check was for $6200 and it has put your account into an overdraft situation. Can you get us a check for $2500 by 2:00 PM?" I was stunned. My mind was racing. I knew that I did not have $2500, but I also knew that I would have to find $2500 by 2:00 PM, because I certainly didn't want to bounce a check to my new landlord. I took a deep breath and said, "No problem. I'll have it to you before two." At that point, it was approximately 11:00 AM.

I immediately went into "crisis mode". I knew I had to think quickly and act efficiently. My first call was to American Express. I decided to ask for an advance on my credit line, even though I knew that I had never applied for the necessary PIN. Their answer was no. The clock ticked as I asked for the supervisor and the supervisor's supervisor. They refused to help. They were happy to provide a PIN so that I could get the money tomorrow, but not today. I finally gave up and decided to go to the next card in my wallet. The same scenario happened. I was put on hold numerous times, talked to every supervisor who would talk to me, and still no results. After repeating this scenario several times, I finally hung up the phone, stared at the pool and said to myself, "Whoa. I am in big trouble. I honestly don't have any way to get **any** money right now."

Just as the situation seemed to have become completely hopeless, I heard a little voice in my head: "Just manifest it." I felt like I had been hit over the head! What was I thinking? In that moment, I fearlessly shifted into "miracle mode" and reminded myself that anything is possible.

I proceeded to create a vision of myself happily walking into the bank and handing the teller a deposit for $2500. In my vision, I greeted the teller and asked her to credit the deposit as soon as possible. I walked out of the bank and checked my watch. It was right before 2:00 PM. I relived that vision a few times, completely believing that it would manifest, and then just "let it go."

I remember sitting there thinking, "Okay, now what do I do?" I reminded myself of the rule for situations like this: "just do the next thing." Since I couldn't think of any other options, I decided to try again to convince American Express to give me the advance.

Moments later, as I was again pleading with a supervisor's supervisor, the call-waiting on my phone beeped. I asked the Amex supervisor to hold for a moment and took the other call. "Hi, Clardy, it's Susan from Westinghouse. Did you move?" I quickly replied, "Hey, Susan, yes, I did move, but can I call you back? I've got a little situation here that I have to take care of." She hung up and I went back to the American Express supervisor, as I wrote "Call Susan @ Westinghouse" on my notepad. I stayed with my call to American Express for another few minutes, but finally I realized that nothing I could say was going to change their rules. They just weren't going to help me.

I hung up and just stared out the window. I couldn't believe that my check to my landlord was probably going to bounce. Everything had been so perfect. I took a deep breath and reviewed my vision one more time before deciding that I didn't have a clue what to do next. It was at that point that I noticed the note about Susan's call. I remember thinking, "Well, you might as well get back to your work, because you've definitely hit a wall. You'll just have to deal with it." I was still shaking my head as I dialed Susan's number. It was almost noon.

"This is Susan."

"Hey, Susan, it's Clardy, what's up?"

"Did you move?"

"Yeah! I found the coolest house in Santa Monica; you've got to come see it. You'll love it. So what's up?"

"Well, we got your check back. I guess they didn't forward it."

"My check? What check?"

"Your royalty check."

"What royalty check?"

"You know, the television royalties from South Africa. That TV special you did."

"We sold the show to South Africa? When did we do that?"

"At the convention in New Orleans. Did you forget?"

"Honestly, Susan, I don't have a clue what you're talking about, but hey, that's great!"

"So where should I send the check?"

"Well...uh...how much is it?"

"Around twenty-five."

(At this point, I am completely astonished! I don't want to sound eager, but I don't know if she's talking about twenty-five cents or twenty-five dollars or twenty five hundred dollars! I decide to play it cool.)

"Oh, great. Let me ask you something, Susan, is there any chance that you guys have a messenger service?"

"Funny you should ask. I have a pouch right here that I'm getting ready to send to Santa Monica."

"Would you mind throwing it in the pouch? Four-twenty-four Fourteenth Street. And...uh... Susan...how much did you say that check was for?"

"Do you want me to open it and give you the exact figure?"

"Do you mind?"

"Twenty-five hundred thirty dollars and sixty-four cents."

"Great! I really appreciate this, Susan. Thanks for your help."

At approximately 1:15, my doorbell rang and I was handed an envelope. Completely in awe, I opened it and stared at the check—$2530.64, even a little more than I needed! Within thirty minutes, my vision played out exactly as I had seen it. I walked into the lobby of the Security Pacific Bank on 15th Street, greeted my favorite teller, and handed her the deposit. She assured me that it would be credited immediately. As I walked back to my car, I smiled and checked my watch—a little before 2:00 PM.

Chapter Two

HOW DOES IT WORK?

Can It Really Be This Simple?

Chapter Two

HOW DOES IT WORK?

Can It Really Be This Simple?

We are what we think.
All that we are arises with our thoughts.
With our thoughts we make our world.
Buddha

What you see is what you get.
What you saw is what you've got.
Clardy Malugen

There's a lot of misinformation out there about the Law of Attraction. It seems that many of the writers and teachers just don't quite explain the whole concept. Millions of people are trying to change their lives with visualization, but the results aren't happening. All of those miracles they were expecting don't seem to be materializing. They may have a few small successes here and there, but the big stuff just isn't happening. So what's wrong?

It's all about energy. In my work, I clearly differentiate between two possible energy states: the *light* and the *cesspool*. The important information here is that there are only **two** states—you're living in one state or the other, there's no in-between.

The light is a place of positive energy. When your energy is rooted in *the light*, you're living in *the moment*, or *the now*. The light is the realm of your authentic self and all of its magnificence. You feel joy, peace, prosperity, gratitude, abundance—all of the good things that reflect who you are—at your core. The light is also the source of all miracles, all positive manifestations. The light is your power place.

When you're functioning from the light, you can easily say, "I feel good," and mean it. The light is all about *feeling good*. It's about being in tune with all of the positive emotions—and being in tune with the natural flow of creative energy.

If you are struggling in any way, your energy is stuck in that other place: the *cesspool*. You are clearly **not** in the *moment*. When you're in the *cesspool*, you are focused on and feeling bad about things in the past, or feeling fear about things that haven't even happened yet—things in an imaginary future where you see yourself as a victim. The cesspool is **not** your power place. When you're in the cesspool, you can't honestly say, "I feel good," because nothing in the cesspool feels good.

Here's the bottom line: when you're in the *cesspool*— or, conversely, not *in the light*—you have given away your power. You're living your life on autopilot. You are allowing yourself to be a victim of each and every negative thought that pops into your mind. As your autopilot responds to these negative thoughts and feelings, you automatically send out negative energy vibrations. The result? You're blindly allowing the potential miracles in your life to be created from a place of negative energy. You are giving up the controls to an unaware ego state—a negative energy state that can only magnetize things like chaos, conflict, anger, depression, boredom—all of the things that you don't enjoy experiencing. All of the things that you would obviously stop creating, if you could just become aware and take back the controls.

Here's the truth about the Law of Attraction: it's all about your energy. You can create the most brilliant affirmations of all time. You can design a vision board that is an exquisite work of art. You can painstakingly produce brilliant audios, movies, and photo albums of your vision. These are all great tools, but if the majority of the time your energy is coming from a negative, chaotic place, you probably won't be manifesting your miraculous vision. You're much more likely to manifest more chaos.

How could this happen? Because instead of providing the universal field with a clear, focused vision about what you would like to create, you are providing *static* the majority of the time. You are automatically putting out chaotic energy into the universal field when you are in an unaware, chaotic state. This energy will brilliantly, powerfully magnetize similar energy right back at you—in other words, more chaos, more static. It will also delay your chances of manifesting your true desires. Is that what you want?

If you want to create conscious miracles, your energy state must support the vision of your miracle.

If your overall energy vibration is primarily coming from a negative, chaotic place, you're making it almost impossible for your positive, life-affirming visions to be magnetized to you. Instead, you are just magnetizing more negativity and chaos.

Here's a great example: one of my clients was sure he wanted a new career, but he just couldn't stop himself from talking about how much he disliked his current job. He constantly focused his energy on the negative situations that he encountered every day at work: unhappy co-workers, belligerent clients, exhausting hours with no appreciation, and so on. Instead of placing his energy on our carefully-crafted vision of his wonderful new career, he blindly chose to waste his energy reliving the negativity that he said he wanted to eliminate! As a result, he was unknowingly attracting more negative situations into his life, not the exciting new career that he had envisioned so carefully.

So how did we shift his energy? We knew that we had to turn off the autopilot that kept him stuck reliving the negative situations. He clearly had an unconscious addiction to an old victim/martyr pattern that was not only running his life, but draining an enormous amount of his energy. To help us "untangle and outsmart" his pattern, we created a very different vision of his current job, so that he could more easily let go of the past and move on to his exciting new career.

In his new vision, co-workers were supportive and friendly, clients were delighted with everything he did, and he worked a lighter, more self-affirming schedule. I gave him the assignment of focusing on this new vision every time he felt himself starting to focus on things that had gone wrong. As days went by, he focused more energy on the positive vision and less on the negative. And, yes, a miracle happened! He was finally free to let go of the negativity and use his energy to create a career that he truly loved.

You're probably wondering how his new career miraculously appeared, right? Well, it appeared perfectly, as all miracles do, just not as he might have planned! As he shifted his own negative energy, it seemed like everything around him also shifted. His co-workers suddenly became friendly and supportive, his clients became more appreciative, and he found himself working less hours and accomplishing more. He started to remember why he had loved his work so much, and decided to re-commit to the wonderful career that he was born to pursue. A simple shift in his energy had led him right back to where he most wanted to be.

Here's the bottom line: you **must** be aware of the energy that you are sending out. If you want to magnetize positive miracles into your life, you **must** make every attempt to keep your energy clear, focused, and positive. Clear, focused, positive energy is rewarded with magical miracle manifestations. Time after time after time. Guaranteed.

Missi's Miracle

In my ongoing seminars, I often give the group an assignment to manifest something—just for practice. I do these *experiments* because it's much easier to manifest when there are no emotional ties or beliefs to get in the way. Once my students are successful at manifesting something that they aren't attached to emotionally, it's much easier to move on to the important stuff. Stuff like new careers, financial success, soulmates, happy families, and the perfect mango.

On the first night of one of my groups, I asked what they'd like to manifest for our little experiment. They starting calling out random suggestions, eventually settling on "a flying pig." I said, "OK, we'll all manifest a flying pig. And what else?" I didn't seem to be getting any definitive suggestions, so I said, "OK, let's try this...somebody choose a flower." Someone called out, "A rose." I said, "OK, somebody, choose a color." Someone called out, "Purple!" I said, "OK, everybody, your assignment is to manifest a flying pig and purple roses."

Early that evening, I particularly noticed one of the younger participants, Missi. She was not only a beautiful human being, but she was so ready to receive this information and so trusting and excited to *go for the gold*. I remember thinking that she was going to be one of the "stars" of this group and that it would be fun to watch her progress. In less than twenty-four hours, I received an excited e-mail from Missi. I'm quoting it below, with her permission:

I don't think anyone is going to believe me. I am seriously in awe. I had no idea where I was going to see a purple rose. Out of the blue today I told my brother I was going to see a flying pig and purple roses. He looked at me and asked if I was on drugs. I just giggled. He had no idea what I went to last night.

About two hours later at work (we work together), I got on my computer and again thought, "Where am I going to see this dang purple rose?" As I was drifting off in thought, I looked at the bulletin board to my left, and my mom had put a little note up of encouragement on the bulletin board with a push pin from I don't even know how long ago. I read it out loud. "No act of kindness is ever wasted," or something like that. Anyway, guess what was surrounding the quote??? PURPLE ROSES!!! Wait it gets better...

I had just gotten home and I was telling my mom the story. I was holding my son and I looked to the right in my mom's room and guess what is hanging from her TV stand??? A CERAMIC FLYING PIG!!

It gets better. I couldn't believe I saw it. I thought... you have got to be kidding me. I had major goose bumps at this point...my mom takes the pig down and you're not going to believe this...it has two purple roses on it!!! My mom goes on to tell me I gave her the pig when I was younger because she used to collect angels. It is a pig with angel wings and purple roses.

Sorry this is so long but I hope you sense my excitement and my details help you understand my awe...And all I did was say out loud: "I am going to see a flying pig and purple roses!"

This is fun.

Although Missi's story will always be one of my favorites, by the end of this particular group, we had manifestation stories about flying pigs and purple roses from **every** participant.

Chapter Three

FOUR MORE LITTLE WORDS

Chapter Three

FOUR MORE LITTLE WORDS

You create your own universe as you go along.
Winston Churchill

Here's the crux of the matter: remember what we said earlier about the Law of Attraction? Remember how we distilled it all down to five little words?

I'll repeat them here:

Ask and you will receive.

OK, now I'm going to treat you to four more little words. If you can truly grasp this concept right here, right now, you'll be free to easily create whatever miracles you can imagine. Ready?

You are <u>always</u> asking.

Get it?

One more time…

You are <u>always</u> asking.

Every day. Every moment. Get it?

It's so simple. Without delving deeply into quantum physics here, let's just say that your energy is always letting the universal energy field know what you want to magnetize to your life. Always. Your personal energy is always signaling the universal field about what you'd like your next step to be. In other words, you're always asking.

OK, now that you've got that, let's take it one step further. You are always asking and…

The universe is always saying <u>yes</u>.

Let's step back for a moment and try to understand this from *the field's* point of view. Imagine that the universal field, spirit, zone, Divine Mother, creative energy—call it whatever you like—is set up to send back to you whatever request you send to it/him/her. Remember…"ask and you will receive"? Remember… "all your prayers will be answered"? You put out the energy automatically and the universal receiver receives your energy. The universal field is absolutely committed to making sure that you receive what you ask for, so it simply goes about sending back that energy vibration, in a similar form.

I know we're talking hybrid physics here, but I want to make it as simple as possible. In other words, in every second of your life, your energy and your thoughts are sending out signals about what you want. And the universal field is helping you create exactly what you're signaling. If you put out negative energy, from a negative, unaware place, the universe doesn't judge that energy; it just goes about sending you what you've ordered. Presto! Alakazam!

Here's another way to look at this concept: you're always asking <u>and</u> you're always receiving what you ask for. **<u>Always</u>**. In every moment. You can consciously ask the universe for a loving soulmate or you can unconsciously send out negative energy when that guy with the weird bumper sticker cuts you off on the freeway. Either way, you will be getting back what you are putting out. It's your choice.

It is **so** important that you understand this one point: **you are irresistible** to the universal energy. It is **committed** to giving you what you ask for. In every moment. Be vigilant about what you are asking for, because you are going to get it—whatever it is!

I recently created a bumper sticker that says, "**You are irresistible**." I keep a copy right above my desk and in my car. I would strongly suggest that you remind yourself of this fact as often as possible. You truly are irresistible. **Always remember** that you and you alone are responsible for the energy that you are putting out into the universal field. And **always remember** that you are going to attract into your life an exact match for the energy that you are sending out. You aren't just magnetic—you are absolutely irresistible.

It doesn't get much simpler than this—and it doesn't get more profound. Take responsibility for your energy—and miracles will start happening all around you—quickly and efficiently. Guaranteed.

The Duck Miracle

At our website MyMiracleVision.com, we invite members of our community to post manifestation stories. Miraculous is the only way to describe many of these amazing manifestations. I'd like to share a story with you that I posted on the website. This one isn't about millions of dollars or the perfect soulmate, but something about this story is so sweet and so simple that it's become one of my favorites. It's a perfect example of attracting a match for what you're sending out—consciously or unconsciously.

This one is a hoot! I was doing some rewrites on my book and thinking about how amazing it is that we truly do manifest whatever we visualize. I was "in the light," feeling great, so I just said to the universe, "OK, show me something that will make me laugh." As I recall, I promptly moved on and forgot about my request, as the business of the day took over.

Fast forward to that afternoon. I was driving to the grocery store, listening to the radio, and I heard a silly joke about two ducks. Since my kids and I like to tell stupid jokes, I kept repeating this joke in my head, so I wouldn't forget it.

The joke went something like this: "There were two ducks floating down a river. One duck says to the other duck, "QUACK!" The other duck says, "Whoa...I was just gonna say that!"

I thought, "OK! The perfect joke to tell the kids!" So while I was in the grocery store and in the car on the way home and puttering around the house that evening, I **kept** repeating this silly joke in my head. I couldn't get it off my mind. "These two ducks were...." I remember laughing to myself. "There are SO many more important things I could be thinking about and focusing on, but I can't stop seeing and hearing these two silly ducks!"

I'm happy to say that I repeated it enough to remember it perfectly to tell the kids when they got home—of course, they didn't think it was very funny, but that's beside the point!

Fast forward to the next morning. I was up having my coffee and I noticed what appeared to be a big bird by the swimming pool. I told my son, "Wow, look! There's a big bird standing by the pool." Then, as I got a closer look, I realized it was a **duck**! But wait...there were **two** of them!

I was absolutely amazed. I stood there and watched two ducks parade around the pool deck. One jumped into the pool *and swam around. The other one preferred the Jacuzzi, so he just hung out in the Jacuzzi before waddling around the deck. I stood there laughing and just watching them parade around. It was hilarious. Just as I ordered!*

By the way, in the five years that I had lived in my home, there had never been a duck in my backyard. And there hasn't been one since.

Visualize ducks and you get ducks.
Clardy Malugen

Chapter Four

STAY AWAY FROM TV, NEWSPAPERS, NEGATIVE WEBSITES, AND NEGATIVE PEOPLE!

Chapter Four

STAY AWAY FROM TV, NEWSPAPERS, NEGATIVE WEBSITES, AND NEGATIVE PEOPLE!

You must not allow yourself to dwell for a single moment on any kind of negative thought.
Emmet Fox

Our concept of energy management is especially crucial in today's environment. With all of the negative news and fear-based energy that is being focused on in our society, there has never been a more important moment in history to learn these laws of manifestation and learn them quickly.

When you feel your energy sinking into the negative chaos around you, **take control** of your energy and **stop** the negative downward spiral. Shift your energy quickly into a positive space and envision the miracle that you want to manifest. You **can** do this and you **must** do this.

There are so many negative people who choose to "see" the worst-case scenario in our future. The best thing you can do is stay away from them. Believe me, the last thing you want to do is get hung up in someone else's vision of chaos. Why should you let **their** negative energy determine **your** future? Why would you choose to start vibrating right along with their chaos? Do you really want to shift into autopilot and signal the universe to send you more negativity? Of course not!

Remember that there is only one person at the controls in your life—YOU!!! And there is no time like the present moment to change your life and change it dramatically—no matter how bad you think things are. Forget about the worst-case scenario. Let go of your fears. Take the controls and live from your heart! Fill your life with positive people and life-affirming situations. The universe is limitless. You know what you want. Focus on it...and let the miracles begin!

The Vulture Miracle

I recently found myself getting sucked into the negative mind-set around me—and feeling hopeless and confused. As I listened to story after story of "vultures" circling around prime real estate properties and trying to buy them for pennies on the dollar, I found myself worrying about my own investments. I actually caught myself dramatically repeating to someone that "vultures" are out there trying to take advantage of this difficult situation—not a good choice on my part!

Shortly after I caught myself focusing on the "vulture" reference, I decided to take the weekend off and head to the beach to stay in my home on the intracoastal waterway. It felt good to get away from the negative energy surrounding the economic downturn—and take some well-deserved relaxation time. You can imagine my surprise when I noticed a **large** black bird sitting in the driveway of my home. As I drove toward him, he stared in my eyes and then flew up and perched at the center of the garage roof. He sat there, in the very center, like he "owned the place." I was absolutely dumbfounded when I realized that my vision of "vultures" had indeed manifested! I was so focused on the ridiculous "vulture" image that I had actually manifested a real vulture!

I sat in the car and laughed. The vulture just sat on the garage roof staring at me. It was clearly a stand-off. After a while, I decided that I was going to have to face the vulture head-on, because it didn't look like he was going anywhere. I drove the car forward to the garage, gave myself a lecture about letting go of my fears, and opened the door to face the vulture. Of course, he was nowhere to be found. I assume he had flown on to find his "next victim"!

Visualize vultures and you get vultures.
Clardy Malugen

Chapter Five

JUST PLACE
YOUR ORDER

Chapter Five

JUST PLACE YOUR ORDER

*Once you make a decision,
the universe conspires to make it happen.*
Ralph Waldo Emerson

When teaching visualization in my workshops, I often use the metaphor of the restaurant order line with a pick-up window. Although the manifestation process is actually similar, the outcome can be exceedingly more exciting!

When we're dealing with the universal energy, the menu is truly unlimited. Anything that you can imagine is right there for the asking. And even more exciting, you may receive something even more wonderful than what you originally ordered! Imagine that! All you have to do is **decide what you want**. Pretty simple, huh?!

The Universal Café

So here's how it happens: you head on over to the Universal Café to check out the amazing, infinite menu. You imagine what you want, you explore the various possibilities, and, finally, you decide which choice is the one to satisfy your desires perfectly. How do you know which choice is the right one? It's the choice that feels really good. You just **know** that it's right. So, when you've figured it out, you just step up to the window that says, "ORDER HERE".

Place Your Order

How do you place your order? You clearly state to the universe exactly what you want to manifest. We'll cover that more precisely in the next section, but, for now, just make your order as simple and clear as possible. Once you have *proclaimed* your order/desire, it's time to move to the next step.

Invest Your Energy

The next step is what I call the *investment stage*. Once you've asked for what you want, you'll want to invest some clear, focused energy so your order will manifest quickly. In our restaurant metaphor, you'll move to the window that says, "**PAY HERE**."

How do you invest your energy? By placing your energy repeatedly on your vision/desire and following your *hunches* about actions you should take. Remember those times when you just **have** to have that Caesar salad or that blackberry smoothie? You order it and while you're waiting, you vividly imagine what it looks like. You can almost taste it and smell it, right??

That's how it works at the Universal Café. You get a clear picture of what you've ordered and place energy on it while you're waiting. You will also find that you'll have hunches about actions you should take. Those little nudges are the key to manifestation. **Always** follow those hunches. For example, in our Universal Café scenario, you might have a hunch that you'll need a fork to eat your manifested burrito. You take action. You grab a fork so you'll be ready when the order arrives. Simple stuff...but always follow through.

You'll be delighted and amazed at where these hunches will lead you. Whenever you have an intuitive hunch that originates in positive energy, just follow it. By taking these action steps, you are proclaiming to the universe that you **believe** that your desire will manifest and that you are ready to receive. The universe likes that sort of thing, and will respond promptly!

Prepare to Receive

OK…you've ordered, you've paid, you've invested your energy, you've followed your hunches, you've taken action, and you're ready to receive. It's time to move to the next window: "**PICK UP ORDER HERE.**"

But wait, let's digress for a moment…think about the last time you experienced a line like this. Once you had placed and paid for your order, did you stand there and worry about whether it was going to be waiting at the pick-up window? Did you get fearful and depressed at the possibility that it might not show up? Did you take the opportunity to beat yourself up a little and ask yourself if you truly deserved to receive your order? Did you get nervous and anxious about whether everyone else in line was going to get his/her order and you weren't going to get yours?

Did you? Of course not. Why? Because you simply trusted the process. You placed your order, invested your money/energy, and expected your order to be waiting, exactly as you ordered it. The universe is like that. It always comes through. Remember those five little words: "ask and you will receive." It's way too simple. But that's the way it works. Every time. It couldn't be more simple. But I digress—

So, you've made it to the pick-up window. You're delighted to see your order sitting there waiting for you—exactly as you ordered it. You calmly, happily, receive your order, and feel blessed that you can now enjoy it. You take a moment to look the Universal Café clerk right in the eye. You say, "Thanks! This is **wonderful**! It's even better than I imagined!"

That's it. You did it. Congratulations!

The Typewriter Miracle

Years ago, when I was starting my career in New York, I often did temp work for companies like ABC Television and MGM Entertainment. I had been a writer for years, and my excellent typing skills came in handy during my pre-computer "starving artist" days. I loved the excitement of working in the big skyscrapers, but most of all, I loved being able to type on IBM Selectric typewriters. Back then, they were the best of the best. For me, the opportunity to use an IBM Selectric was absolute bliss, especially since my own typewriter was a cheap little portable with keys that stuck about half of the time.

The more I worked on the IBM Selectric, the more I wanted one of my own. I wanted that typewriter so badly, but I couldn't begin to imagine how I could afford to get one. I tried to research older, used ones, but they were still too expensive—and, frankly, I didn't want an old model. Weeks went by with daydreams about my IBM Selectric until one night my old "manifestation" light bulb went off. "Wait a minute," I thought. "I'll just manifest one!"

I determined that I would have my own IBM Selectric typewriter and that it would be **free**! I didn't know where it was coming from, but I knew it was **mine**! I created a vision of walking to my front door and seeing a large box. I saw myself opening the box and unpacking my very own IBM Selectric typewriter. I saw myself typing on my IBM Selectric and smiling at how amazing it was that it had manifested for **free**!

I continued to focus on my vision often, but weeks went by and still no IBM Selectric typewriter. As time went by, I started doubting myself and the whole manifestation process. Maybe a free IBM Selectric was a bigger miracle than I was capable of!

I was sitting in my apartment that fateful morning, attempting to type on my pathetic old portable, telling myself to "Just get over it!" when the phone rang. It was my mother. She said, "Clardy, do you still need a typewriter?" I said,

"Yeah, I do, but I was hoping for a certain kind of typewriter. Why do you ask?" Well, your brother has an old typewriter that he doesn't need. He said he would give it to you. Just call him if you want it."

I hung up and thought to myself, "Just go ahead and take the typewriter. It's a very generous offer. You're crazy to think you can get an IBM." I debated with myself about my manifestation plan. If I took his typewriter, would that undermine my chances for manifesting the IBM? Would I be settling for mediocrity when there was still a chance that the universe would bring me my heart's desire? My rational mind took the lead. I decided that I would be crazy not to accept his typewriter since my old portable was truly on its last legs. I called my brother.

"Hey, I heard you had an old typewriter that you don't need."

"Yeah, one of my clients is in financial trouble. He's closing his office and he offered to give me a typewriter to apply against the bill."

"Really? What kind is it?"

"An IBM Selectric. Have you ever used one?"

"You're kidding."

"No, why?"

"You're offering me an IBM Selectric typewriter?"

"Yeah. You want it?"

"Are you kidding? Of course I want it."

"You want to just get the next time you're here, or should I ship it to you?"

"Can you ship it?"

"Sure. We can ship it out tomorrow."

Three days later, a big box arrived at my door. In that box was an IBM Selectric typewriter. A **free** IBM Selectric Typewriter. I unpacked it and placed it on my desk right in the spot that had been waiting for it. And yes, it was bliss!

Chapter Six

ASK FOR WHATEVER YOU WANT

Chapter Six

ASK FOR WHATEVER YOU WANT

Follow your bliss and the Universe will open
doors where there were only walls.
Joseph Campbell

I'd have to say that over 90 percent of my seminar participants and private clients come to me complaining that they don't have a clue what they want. I don't know how many times I've heard the words, "That's the problem. I just don't know what I want." My response to that comment is always the same. "Of course you know what you want. Everyone knows what they want. You're just too busy focusing on what you don't want. You can't see the roses for the weeds."

They then fight me for a few minutes, telling me every reason, every excuse for why they don't know what they want. There are some really good excuses, by the way. I'm pretty sure I've heard them all! But the bottom line is this: the magnificent being within you, the <u>you</u> that is truly <u>you</u> at your core, knows **exactly** what it wants. Whatever problem or challenge you are currently facing, you intuitively know the perfect outcome. Just trust me on this one. Take a deep breath and take a moment to bask in the light of your own magnificence. From that vantage point, you will not only know what you want, you will immediately start taking the steps to get there.

That being said, if you're having trouble basking at the moment, we can try the back door. With so much negative energy out there these days, I know how hard it can be to disassociate yourself from the distress and the chaos. If you need a miracle in your life right now, let's just calmly figure out what the perfect miracle would be and go about making it happen. And let's have some fun while we're doing it!

Here's what we'll do:

Focus on the area of your life that you'd most like to shift. Let's say you've lost your job or you're afraid that you might. By the way, when you take a step back from the chaos that you've created around this possibility, you might suddenly realize that you'd actually like to change careers. Wow. What a great opportunity!

OK, so what do you want? Make a list describing the perfect career for you. If you find yourself wanting to talk about the things that you don't want, just reframe every negative into a positive. Think about what would make you happy, what would make you feel good. Put your energy and your focus on happiness and the positive aspects of your new future opportunities.

For example, a recent client was tired of working in what she described as a *boys club* environment. In the workplace, she felt like she was excluded from the decision-making processes. We envisioned a new situation where she was highly respected as part of a dynamic, creative team of individuals who were excited about creating positive outcomes. We chose to focus our energy on this new exciting possibility, rather than rehashing the negatives of her current situation. And, sure enough, a headhunter somehow *found* her, after what seemed like a miraculous coincidence. But, sorry, no coincidences here...just the universe doing its thing.

One of my favorite career stories is about a dear friend who was getting hit with changes in just about every area of her life. She came to me discouraged and very concerned about her future. Her job had ended, she was on unemployment, her divorce was final, and she was facing a new beginning unlike anything she had ever experienced.

As she frantically sent out resumes, I suggested that we focus on getting a clear vision of what she wanted for a new career. She kept saying that she didn't really know exactly what she wanted to do, so I suggested that she make a list of the things that she did know.

Her list went something like this: she wanted to do something creative, she wanted to make more money than she had been making, she wanted an office with a window, she wanted to work with interesting people, and she wanted to have a candy dish on her desk so that people would stop by all day and say hello. That's all that she was sure of, but that was enough. At the time that we started focusing our energy on these things, neither of us had any idea what she was going to be doing or where the job would be located. We just visualized the items on the list and excitedly anticipated the results.

A couple of weeks later, a woman that she had worked with several years before called out of the blue and asked her to come to interview for a production assistant position at one of the top animation studios in the country. The rest is history.

She started a new career in animation, complete with the now-infamous candy dish, and has progressed up the ladder to a high-powered position working with some of the top animation directors in the world. The candy dish, alas, is no longer on her desk. She's now too busy to chat. The candy dish has been moved to the kitchen of the new home that she manifested using these methods and she now enjoys candy with her new boyfriend...yet another manifestation story!

These simple techniques work equally well for magnetizing money, relationships, weight release, new homes, paid-off mortgages, whatever you want. The lesson here is that you don't have to know exactly what your new career might be. You don't have to know your future soulmate's middle name or what color socks he or she wears—unless that's truly important to you! You just have to know some of the details about what **you want**.

What do you love? What makes you feel good? What puts a smile on your face—and a glow in your heart? Ask yourself these questions, write down the answers, and then go about asking the universe for whatever you truly desire. The universe will figure out how to deliver! And you'll love it when it arrives!

The Guest House Miracle

Years ago, I was a visiting professor at a university in Miami, Florida. At the time, the population of Miami was rising quickly and housing was very difficult to find. After searching unsuccessfully for several days when I first arrived into town, I was offered a temporary roommate situation while I looked for something more suitable. I was grateful for the offer, and moved in. Weeks went by and I looked at apartment after apartment, utilizing every channel that I could think of. I seemed to find nothing but properties in need of repair, in unsafe areas, and so on. Weeks turned into months, and I was truly ready give up.

I remember sitting in my small bedroom that night, staring at the wall, trying to figure out what to do next. Suddenly, my "light bulb" went off and I reminded myself that I had never bothered to "ask" for what I really wanted. I immediately grabbed a notebook and a pen and started making a list describing my perfect situation. Since I'd been searching all over Miami, I was very clear that I preferred to live in Coral Gables, a beautiful, charming area. My list began with: a guest house behind a beautiful home in Coral Gables—which seemed impossible at the time, but I was going for "perfect"! The list continued as follows: $350 a month, no long-term lease, fully furnished in a way that I love, a pretty, outdoor patio by a pool, and lots of beautiful, tropical landscaping. From that list, I created a vision of myself at my wonderful guest house, sitting on the patio amid all of the beautiful plants, grateful for my beautiful living situation. I remember feeling positive about my vision and honestly believing that it would come to pass. I laid the notebook by my bed and fell asleep.

I woke up the next morning, still feeling good about my vision, and proceeded to the kitchen to make coffee. I noticed a copy of the Miami Herald sitting on the kitchen table— already open to the classified section. (As an aside, I was never able to identify who placed the paper there). I sat down with my coffee and looked down to see the "For Rent" section, as I had done for months, and was very surprised to see an ad that I had not seen before. It read: Apartment for Rent, $350/month, no lease, fully furnished. I remember thinking that it was odd to see a new ad on Saturday, but I immediately dialed the number. A woman with a British accent answered the phone. I asked first if the apartment was still available. She responded that she had just placed the ad and that I was the first person to call. I asked her if she could tell me a little bit about it. She replied, "It's actually a guest house behind our home. It's fully furnished, with a little patio. The rent is $350 per month and we prefer a month to month lease." I was stunned as I asked, "Can you tell me where it is located?" She replied that it was in Coral Gables and gave me the street address. I immediately set up an appointment for later that morning to view the property.

As I drove through Coral Gables that morning, I was incredulous that my vision seemed to be coming true. I remember telling myself that I shouldn't expect too much...that just living in Coral Gables would be great. As I pulled up in front of the house, I was stunned at how beautiful the neighborhood was and how beautiful the home was. I rang the bell and the owner pointed me to a private entrance on the side and asked me to walk through that gate and to the back of the home. I was again stunned to open the gate and find what could only be described as a tropical paradise. A stone path led through a beautifully landscaped backyard with exotic plants and fountains. The large pool enclosure also served as the home to five pairs of tropical birds. It was truly remarkable and utterly breathtaking. The universe had led me to a guest house on the property of a couple who owned a tropical plant distribution company!

My future home was exactly what I had ordered. Fully furnished with wonderful artwork from their African travels, an adorable patio, $350/month, and no long-term lease. I quickly moved in and was grateful every day that I had been blessed with such a wonderful place to live.

Chapter Seven

HOW TO ASK

Chapter Seven

HOW TO ASK

Whatsoever ye shall ask in prayer,
believing, ye shall receive.
Matthew 21:22 King James Bible

The *how* of manifestation is about visualization, clearly focusing your energy, and believing with every fiber of your being that your desires will manifest. Never forget that "you are irresistible" to the universal energy. As you work with the concept of energy management, you'll find that you'll have more energy to focus in ways that will truly make a difference in your life. Once you take back control of your energy, you can utilize it to attract what you truly desire. This, of course, is that same energy that you formerly utilized to create chaos in your life. You'll like this a lot better. Trust me.

The key to all of these occurrences lies in the practice of what I call **Magnetic Visualization**. It's a type of creative visualization that fully utilizes all five senses and helps you manifest more quickly and powerfully than other visualization methods. Let's take a moment to go over "The Seven Secrets of Magnetic Visualization."

THE

Seven Secrets

OF

MAGNETIC
VISUALIZATION

Secret #1

Acknowledge your desire as clearly as possible—
with **no** limits.

Secret #2

Create a clear intention that
will satisfy your desire.

Secret #3

State your intention as a vision
that has **already** manifested
in the **present** time.

Secret #4

Choose a very special moment from your future
vision and live it fully—empowering it with all of
your senses.

Secret #5

Proclaim your vision to the universe often—by writing, speaking and visualizing.

Secret #6

Expect a miracle. Acknowledge all hunches, signals, omens, and coincidences. Take every action that you feel "led" to take.

Secret #7

Enjoy your manifestation.
Celebrate your success.
Give thanks.

Secret #1

Acknowledge your desire as clearly as possible—with **no** limits.

To get started, describe your desire as precisely as possible. Remember that there are no limits. Let me say that again...there are truly **no** limits to what you can magnetize to yourself. Allow your imagination to run free and come up with the perfect statement of your desire.

That being said, getting clear about your desire is one of the fastest ways to reveal your self-imposed limitations. I love to push people to *pump up the volume* with their desires, but I never push them past what they believe to be their true self-imposed limitations. You need to believe that you can manifest your desire, and not try to magnetize something that is out of your realm of believability. And this is truly an individual belief.

Self-imposed limitations are never more evident than when there is a large group of people working with the concept of money. Everyone wants to manifest more money, but it is so enlightening to see the differences in the amounts of money that each person sees as a possibility. One person thinks that $500 is impossible, but he can easily work with manifesting $250. The next person is fine with $10,000, but don't ask her to go for $50,000, and so on. If you don't believe you can manifest something, you will be prone to putting more energy on *disbelief*, which will immediately sabotage your efforts. So make your desire believable and, as you experience success with your efforts, you can stretch your ability to believe in bigger and better things. Time and success will support you in the ultimate realization that you truly can manifest **anything** that your heart desires. There's no reason to rush it, the proof will come.

One of my favorite examples of *stating your desire* comes from a workshop a few years back. I often ask people to begin the manifestation practice by starting with something simple, a common item that they would truly like to have. Although other participants were calling out things like soulmates, Porsches, and lottery winnings, David, one of the first-timers, stated that he really wanted a nice new vacuum cleaner. As laughter erupted all over the room, David emphatically stated that he was tired of his rug being dirty and he knew exactly what kind of vacuum cleaner he wanted. I remember thinking in that moment that there was no question in my mind that David would manifest that vacuum cleaner. He was so powerfully clear about his desire and his expectation that it would manifest.

As the day went on, the vacuum cleaner became a symbol of sorts and was mentioned repeatedly. However, as the day progressed, it also became evident that a vacuum cleaner wasn't exactly what David really desired. As David's energy got clearer, we realized that what David really wanted was a clean house! So David's vision became that he wanted to attract the perfect housekeeper to keep his home sparkling clean. His new vision of the perfect housekeeper replaced his desire for the perfect vacuum cleaner. But I remember thinking that a lot of *vacuum cleaner* energy had already been put out into the universe and that it wouldn't surprise me if the vacuum cleaner somehow arrived also!

I will never forget what happened when I got home from that workshop. I was excited and thrilled with the results of the day, but physically exhausted from the energy that I had expended. I grabbed my dinner, sunk into the chaise by the television, and hit the "on" button on the remote. By some *strange* coincidence, the channel was tuned to the Home Shopping Network, and, you've guessed it, onscreen I saw the most amazing ten-piece vacuum cleaner set that I have ever seen!

By the way, a few weeks later, David happily reported that he had manifested a wonderful housekeeper **and** a great new vacuum cleaner.

The lesson here is: always state your desire as clearly as possible, but be open to taking that desire a step further. Open your mind and your heart so that you can imagine an even greater manifestation of your desire—whether it's the perfect housekeeper or the man of your dreams! As you work with these concepts, it will get easier to allow yourself exactly what you **truly** desire.

And, for the record, David went on to huge successes with his new talent at magnetic visualization. He manifested a new job, a new home, a new relationship, and lost forty pounds—all within a few months!

Secret #2

Create a clear intention that will satisfy your desire.

Now that you have identified your desire, you'll need to turn that desire into a very clear **intention**. This step is an important logistical step that is designed to help you get to the next, more important step.

For example, "I will have a new housekeeper who comes twice a week and is great with my laundry." Or "I will increase my sales by thirty-five percent within six months." Or "I will sell my home within three months and move into a lakefront home." Or "I will meet the woman of my dreams and marry her this year."

What we're doing here is getting clear about exactly what it is that we **intend** to happen. We acknowledge to ourselves that not only is our vision possible…it **will** happen. It often takes this step for people to get acquainted with the possibility that they really **can** manifest whatever they desire. As this point, if you have doubts about your ability to manifest your vision, you can adjust your vision so that it enters into the realm of believability for you. Again, be very sure that your intention **feels** possible to you. If you create an intention that you can't seem to feel good about, just adjust your intention until it feels good. Sometimes just making the intention **fun** will take care of the problem.

In one of my workshops years ago, one of the women was experiencing a difficult financial situation. When it came time to practice *creating intentions*, her intention was simple, but clear: "I will have a car within a month." As I sensed her energy state, it was obvious that this woman was not one of those students who was envisioning a red Porsche convertible. Her future vision of car ownership was more about a vehicle that had tires and worked well enough to get her to her job.

As an aside, let me reiterate that although I am certain that **anything** is possible, that truth is just not believable yet to many people. Although I always push my students to expand their beliefs so that they eventually discover for themselves that we live in a limitless universe, I never push them into a place that does not feel believable to them. My work has taught me that everyone who follows these concepts will eventually *get it*. It takes only a couple of miracles to set them straight. And, if they follow the path, the miracles are guaranteed to happen. They always do.

So, let's get back to my story about the woman who wanted a car... When I saw her intention written on her paper, I looked into her eyes, popped her with a hit of positive energy and said, "Wouldn't it be fun to manifest a **free** car?" She jumped right in with me, laughed, and said, "Yeah, that sounds great!" Magnetizing a free car was suddenly exciting to her—and happily within the realm of possibility for her. Her intention now became: "I will have a **free** car within a month." Her energy had shifted, her eyes were sparkling, and she was ready to play the game of magnetizing that free car! You and I both know that creating a **free** car is definitely shifting into the realm of miracles, but she was fine with it, clear about her intention, and ready to move on to making it happen.

The lesson here is that as long as your intention feels right to you—go for it! What may seem impossible to everyone around you may be exactly the perfect intention for you.

By the way, a couple of weeks after that workshop, I got an e-mail from her—it was one of those bizarre coincidence stories about a friend of a relative who no longer had a place to park an extra car that he had... long story short, she was now the proud owner of a car.

Not just a car, by the way, but a *free* car! So...state your intention clearly, make sure it feels good to you, and move to the next step.

Secret #3

State your intention as a vision that
has **already** manifested in the **present** time.

Now that you have identified what you want and stated it as an intention, it's time to get down to the business of making your intention a reality!

You'll want to **place your energy** on exactly what you want to manifest. Don't ever forget that the energy of your vision is magnetic. As you begin to place energy on your new vision, the universe will already be maneuvering to make your desire a reality.

Here's the key: simply state your intention as a vision that has already manifested in the present time. Take the desire from *"I want"* to *"I'm already there enjoying it."*

You'll need to clearly show the universe exactly what you want—as if it has already manifested. For example, if you'd like to manifest a new home, you would *see* yourself in your joyful future and you'd state from your heart: "I love living in my beautiful new home." This step is incredibly powerful in opening your energy to the new vision. Your world will immediately expand as you imagine and state the present truth of your future manifestation. Simply put, something wonderful happens energetically when you move into this place of innocent belief. You're setting yourself up for a magical response from the universe.

Let me take a moment to repeat something. In the previous paragraph, you were instructed to take your desire from *"I want"* to *"I'm already there enjoying it."* Notice that I didn't just say, *"I'm already there."* The key phrase is *"I'm already there enjoying it."* Your future vision must contain the statement of your positive **feelings** that surround the creation of your vision. Don't miss this point. When you're feeling **positive** about your future manifestation, your energy is strong and vibrant—and it will bring your vision into reality much faster and more easily.

By the way, don't ever make the mistake of sending out energy of *wanting* something. You'll manifest more *wanting*. Always send out grateful energy that is clear about exactly what you have *already manifested*. It's very simple, very clean, very precise. Keep it that way.

I often have students who have studied creative visualization before. They usually want to try to make lists and let it go at that. Lists are fine if they are used as part of the process of getting you clear about what you truly desire. They are only a means to an end. Stating your vision isn't about making a list. It's about creating a simple statement that says clearly what you desire. If you like to write out long descriptions of your future job or future home or future partner, there is nothing wrong with that, but ultimately you'll need to take that description a step further. You'll want to *own it* and *live it*, as you'll see in the next step.

Secret #4

Choose a very special moment from your future vision and **live it fully**—empowering it with all of your senses.

This is the most important step of all. The energy that is attached to all of your senses is the key to attracting your desires quickly and easily. If you'd like your visions to manifest at warp speed, you'll simply need to engage **all** of your senses.

If you think about it, right here, right now, in this moment, you are fully immersed in that amazing environment that we call the *now*. Your senses are fully functioning. (If one or more of your senses is impaired, the others are probably making up for it.) Take a moment to ask yourself what your senses are communicating to you right now. What are you seeing, touching, tasting, smelling, hearing...?

As I'm sitting here, I can feel the cool air against my skin. I love the way that my new keyboard feels and the soft sounds it makes when my fingers hit the keys. I can hear the wind blowing outside. I see the wind whipping the sails of a gorgeous sailboat that is heading south past my home on the intracoastal waterway. I see the letters as I type them. They are the perfect size and the perfect font. I am immersed in a sensory experience that is **very** rich. As I write this, I am so grateful to be in the *now*, experiencing this beautiful environment, and doing something that I love so much. I feel so blessed! Frankly, that's what it always feels like when you're firmly placed in the *now*, but I digress. Whoa...here comes another sailboat... gorgeous! OK...back to you.

Take a moment, right here, right now, to experience your present moment fully. You can hear whatever is going on around you, you can feel the air against your skin, and you can see these words and whatever is around you at the moment. There is a taste in your mouth. There is a smell in the air, maybe the scent of a flower or the aroma of coffee brewing. Feel it all. Analyze it all for a moment. Make sure you've experienced each of your senses and all of them together. Now do it again. Can you feel that? Now do it again.

OK? Did you get that? Your future vision needs to feel just like that. All the senses engaged.

Now here's a key concept: by now, you should have a pretty good idea of what you want your future vision to look and feel like. So take the next step...choose a **very** special moment from a time when your vision has already manifested and visualize that moment. Make it a full, **sensory** experience. Got it? OK!

I'm going to repeat this one more time. Choose a **very** special moment from a time when your vision has already manifested and **visualize that moment**. Make it a full, sensory experience. That's it. That's all that you have to do. That moment, that sensory-filled expression of your manifested desire, will actually create your desire. You just have to place your energy on it and watch it happen. It's truly that simple!

If you have trouble choosing your special moment, you may want to consider moments that are special celebrations, like anniversaries or birthdays. Those kinds of moments are already full of excitement and positive energy and are easy to visualize.

I often tell the story of my vision of my future children. It's a perfect example. I remember sitting by my pool in Santa Monica, enjoying a beautiful day, grateful for my wonderful home and my exciting career. I was a single woman, thirty-nine years old, and I felt like I was exactly where I wanted to be. And then...a sobering thought came to me, just like the old joke..."Oh, no! I forgot to have kids!" I remember sitting there, thinking that I had obviously manifested pretty much everything else that I wanted. Maybe it was time to manifest the babies. So I set out to do just that!

So, let's review the procedures. My *desire* was to have two children. My *intention* was: I will have two babies soon. The next step was to create a vision from my future life when my desire had already manifested. I chose to see myself and two babies swimming around in a pool. I felt the sun on my skin and splashes of water hitting my face. I laughed and kicked around underwater with the kids as they splashed me and called me "Mama." My vision lasted all of a few seconds and ended with my saying, "These babies are such a joy!" I placed energy on this vision on and off for several months. I can tell you that as I repeated this vision back then, I absolutely saw and felt that I was right there in that pool with those babies.

In about a year, I was married and expecting my first son. His brother was born when he was eighteen months old. I definitely manifested two *babies*—just like my vision—and plenty of diapers...in two different sizes...and a double stroller...and sleepless nights, for several years. I asked for *babies* and I got *babies!* Of course, it goes without saying that they both love the water and that they're the greatest joy of my life.

Following along in the "be careful what you ask for" vein, it's actually surprising to me now that I didn't have their father in the vision. I was so focused on the babies that I forgot to make sure their father was around. He was nowhere to be seen in my vision at the pool. Unfortunately, our marriage did not last and I learned an important lesson about creating visions!

Remember, once you create the vision of this *empowered* moment from your inevitable future, you're on the way to magnetizing your miracle. The energy of your magical moment, that sensory-filled expression of your manifested desire, will now be able to create your desire.

So let's move on to the next step, putting your vision *out there* in specific, concrete ways.

Secret #5

Proclaim the vision to the universe often—by writing, speaking, and visualizing.

In the beginning, you'll want to *proclaim your vision* often, with lots of energy. What does that mean exactly? Just sending your vision out into the ether, out into the field of all possibilities, out into the universal energy field. You can do that by writing, speaking, or visualizing. Or all three.

This step is all about **owning** your vision, **living** your vision, by engaging your emotions and your senses fully. When you truly own your vision, truly live it, your vision will become irresistible to the universe. It has no choice but to deliver—exactly as you've ordered!

You can always type your visions, but there's something about the physical act of writing that creates an energetic conscious reality. I like to create three-by-five-inch cards with my various visions. I keep the cards around as reminders during the day.

You can also grab a pen every night or every morning and write your visions in a notebook. Another effective method is creating a diary from that future place where your desire has already manifested. I have a beautiful black book that I keep by my bed, and carry in my suitcase wherever I go. I write in it or just review it every chance I get.

Vision boards and photo albums are also wonderful tools. In both cases, you create a concrete representation of your miraculous future. Find photos online or in your favorite magazines and design a visual montage of your upcoming miracles. Place your vision board in a prominent place and focus your energy on it often. Your photo album, entitled "My Miraculous Life", can include page after page of wonderful images of your fabulous new life. You can sit in bed every night and enjoy "reminiscing" about your exciting future. Speaking your desire is also a great way to put the energy out there. When you're creating that *special moment* from your future life that we discussed in the previous section, it's a great idea to create a phrase that encapsulates the vision for you. Remember my sentence: "These babies are such a joy!" The expression of those words always put me right in the vision of the pool and those babies. I made an audio tape of myself speaking those words and listened to it repeatedly in my car. I spoke it aloud and spoke it in my imagination when I heard the tape. Both ways work well.

Whatever your sentence is, make sure it takes you into that place of complete sensory involvement. It doesn't have to be long and complicated. In fact, it's much better if it is simple and to the point. Just grab onto it—see it, feel it, taste it, touch it—and, most importantly, **enjoy** it!

Once you have sent the energy of your vision into the universe by writing, speaking, or visualizing, just take a simple moment to *release* the energy consciously. **Feel** yourself allowing the energy to surge out into the ether. **Know** that the universe is already manifesting your desire for you. **Feel** gratitude that your vision is becoming reality. **Celebrate** the exciting success that is already yours!

This is a very important moment, because you are acknowledging the undeniable reality that your vision is *in process*. It's on the way. It's also important because it allows you to expand your energy and your ability to imagine even more expansive realities for yourself.

To review: use every possible opportunity to place your vision out there. Write, speak, and visualize your miracle several times a day. Maintain your highest, most positive energy state as you invest your energy in your vision. You'll be consciously creating the magnetic charge that will bring your desire home, quickly and efficiently.

And, most importantly, next time you feel yourself succumbing to negative energy of any kind that is suddenly encroaching upon your life, shift into miracle-making mode and focus your energy on your vision. By this simple act, you will have stopped yourself from creating the static that would have held you back and kept you stuck in the cesspool. Instead, you have chosen to move yourself closer to the magical manifestation of your chosen miracle. If you can train yourself to shift into that positive mode every time, your life will shift dramatically—very, very quickly. You'll be amazed at the results.

Secret #6

Expect a miracle. Acknowledge all hunches, signals, omens, and coincidences. Take every action that you feel "led" to take.

Once you have set the energy of your vision in motion, you will need to prepare for its manifestation. Show the universe that you are ready. If you need to change anything about your life to prepare for the manifestation of your vision, do it now! If you're manifesting a new car, get your garage cleaned out. If you're manifesting money, research some investment possibilities or open a new savings account. If you're manifesting a new relationship, plan a surprise trip to the islands with your future partner. Simple acts like these will support your belief in the inevitable outcome.

As your energy moves into a place of *expecting* your vision to become a reality, you will start to feel nudges about things that you need to do. Always follow those hunches. It may seem odd or silly to you at the time, but if you suddenly feel like you need to call an old friend, or drop by a bookstore, just do it. You may want to keep a journal of all of your hunches and coincidences. It's always fun to go back and see how things actually progressed. There are so many wonderful stories of little coincidences that can happen on the way to a miracle. Enjoy the process—have a good time with it!

Secret #7

You did it! Enjoy your manifestation.
Celebrate your success. Give thanks.

You're going to love this part! In that wonderful moment when you realize that your vision has become a reality in your life, you will probably experience an immediate sense of wonder and awe. I usually get chills when my visions manifest. There's that wonderful energy surge that occurs when you're in the moment and you suddenly realize that you're **living** your previous vision.

I remember such a moment a few months ago. I was on a plane with my two sons staring out the window on our approach into the airport at Shanghai. One of my visions for our life included travel all over the world. I was reminded of my previous vision and so grateful that we are able to have these wonderful experiences.

Expressing gratitude for the miracle that has appeared in your life is the obvious next step. If you're in the moment, you'll probably just naturally move into *gratitude*. Expressing gratitude places your energy exactly in that powerful, positive place that attracts even more miracles. Enjoy the moment and all of the miracles that are manifesting around you. In the process, you'll be creating an even more magnificent future.

The DAR Award Miracle

My first memory of visualization occurred when I was about five years old. My mother had taken me to the eighth grade awards ceremony at the local school. I remember sitting in the auditorium, my feet not reaching the floor, peering over the seat in front of me. In the middle of the program, a teacher was introduced to announce the Daughters of the American Revolution award, which was to be given to an outstanding girl in the eighth grade. I watched and listened as they announced the name "Ann Lawson." Since I knew Ann, I felt special as I watched her walk up to the podium to receive her award. As she walked up, my mother leaned over to me and whispered, "You need to win that award when you get older."

I thought that was a great idea! I remember watching Ann and thinking about winning the award myself someday. I will never forget sitting in that uncomfortable wooden auditorium chair imagining my future self walking up those stairs and receiving that award. It felt really good!

Fast forward to my own eighth grade awards ceremony. I was sitting in that same auditorium, in one of those same uncomfortable chairs, except now my feet were easily touching the floor! I watched as the principal, Mr. Long, said, "Now, our American History teacher, Mr. Joy, will announce the DAR Award." In that moment, now years later, I recalled my earlier vision and thought, "Oh, no! I forgot I was supposed to win that award!" My mind was racing as I watched Mr. Joy walk up to the podium. I was kicking myself that I hadn't studied harder and made a better grade in history. If only I hadn't forgotten about the award! I sat there, absolutely riveted to his face, assuming that there was no way he would say my name. But, of course, he announced, "This year's Daughters of the American Revolution Award goes to a very special young lady, Miss Clardy Malugen."

I was stunned as I walked to the stairs and onto the stage to receive my award. It was déjà vu for me. My mother, who was again in the audience, later commented, "What were you thinking about when you went up to receive your award? You looked like you had seen a ghost!"

She, of course, had completely forgotten the words that she had whispered to that little five-year-old girl!

Fast forward once again—to another awards ceremony four years later. I was now sitting in the high school auditorium with the rest of the senior class. You can imagine my shock, toward the end of the program, when I heard the same Mr. Long, now the high school principal, announce that it was time to present the DAR Citizenship Award. I remember thinking, "Oh my gosh, there's another one!" And sure enough, I sat there with chills going down my spine as he announced, "This year's Daughters of the American Revolution Citizenship Award goes to Miss Clardy Malugen." Once again, I walked up the stairs and received the DAR award, just like the vision of that little girl years before, but this time with a huge smile on my face!

Chapter Eight

READY? LET'S DO IT!

Chapter Eight

READY? LET'S DO IT!

Take the first step in faith.
You don't have to see the whole staircase,
just take the first step.
Martin Luther King

OK. Time to get down to business. It's your turn
to create a miracle! Remember, even a five-year-old can
do this stuff! Take a moment to think about what you
would most like to manifest. Choose one thing and
follow the instructions that have just been laid out in
this book.

Keep it simple. Keep your energy positive. When
you're getting tugged into a negative place by things going

on around you—**STOP**!! Replace those negative thoughts with the sensory-rich vision of your soon-to-be-manifested miracle. Place your energy on your vision. See it, feel it, taste it, touch it, revel in it! Dance about it! Giggle about it! What could be more fun than making miracles?

Anyone can do this. Especially you. It's no coincidence that you are reading these words right now. You were led here. You followed your hunches and you followed your heart.

See the next page? It was created especially for your miracle vision. Take a deep breath and get started now.

As you manifest your miracles, you'll be led to the truth of the power within you. You'll intimately begin to feel your connection to the creative energy that links us all. You'll discover the true foundation of your current happiness and experience the limitless possibilities of your exciting new future.

You can create miracles. I am absolutely certain that you can. In fact, I'm visualizing your success right now! ☺

Go get'em, champ! What are you waiting for? Let's manifest miracles!!

My Miracle Vision

by _____

And so it is.

My Miracle Vision

by Clardy Malugen

My mission as a catalyst for personal transformation is
passionately in motion. People across the planet are opening
their hearts and minds to my simple, joyful message. As we
all embrace our true power, miracles are happening
and lives are transforming exponentially.
Each day brings more peace and prosperity to the world as
leaders and citizens unite in positive ways to facilitate change
and uplift the lives of those around them.

My own life is a joyful miracle every day. I live a magnificent
life with my healthy, thriving children and my brilliant,
funny, sexy husband. We travel the world, sharing light and
empowering others. Our beautiful, waterfront home is a
nurturing oasis where we often entertain international leaders,
brilliant artists and thinkers, and the many friends who have
blessed our lives. We enjoy every day to the max by exercising
together, eating healthy, yummy foods, and making each other
laugh. Life is good!

It is remarkable how quickly the energy of our planet
has shifted into a state of "yes".
We all say "yes" to unlimited possibilities.
We say "yes" to brilliantly simple solutions.
We say "yes" to a positive, vibrant new world.

And so it is .

Acknowledgements

My deepest gratitude and love to:

—all of my students and clients, past and present. Thank you for trusting me with your hopes and dreams...and for revealing those pesky hidden "sharks". I am in awe of your courage and delighted with your miracles!

—my beautiful mother, Ethel Malugen, for always assuring me that I could accomplish anything.

—my brother, Joe Malugen, for his kindness and support. Joe, your biggest miracles are yet to come!

—my dear friend, the brilliant psychotherapist, Dr. Peggy Irwin, for her constant support and encouragement. Peg, your wisdom has blessed my life in so many ways.

—my angel band: Lisa Everett, Dr. Christine Jablonski, Sherry Hay, Deborah Sciarrino, Mary Yeager, Ann Furstace, Kim Tarver, Robert Harding, Mark Reisinger, Alex Stelzner, Rosi Bennett, Dr. Isidore DePaula, Lance Avery Morgan, Kimberly Varney, John Stellar, Kate Romero-Stellar, and the administration, faculty, & staff of Trinity Preparatory School.

—my wonderful teenage sons, Dylan and Jamie. I am blessed every day by your laughter, your beautiful music, and your open hearts. Your unconditional love is the sweetest miracle of my life.

—God. It's all about you and always has been. Let's manifest miracles!

Afterword

To find out more about Clardy Malugen, the Prosperity Academy and the Ten Million Miracles Campaign, please visit **www.ProsperityAcademy.com** or **www.ClardyMalugen.com**. Ms. Malugen is available for speaking engagements and individual executive coaching worldwide and is happy to create special programs based on the needs of your organization.

You are invited to participate in the international **Ten Million Miracles Campaign** which has become a catalyst for positive change across the globe. Access the latest information at **www.ProsperityAcademy.com**.

The **Prosperity Academy** offers many opportunities for live and online experiences that can help you achieve the life of your dreams! We look forward to hearing from you and working with you soon!

Wishing you many magnificent miracles—and lots of fun!

Clardy Malugen & the Prosperity Academy Team

www.ProsperityAcademy.com
www.ClardyMalugen.com
Facebook: Clardy Malugen
Twitter: clardym
Blog: clardym.com

About the Author

Clardy Malugen, founder of The Prosperity Academy International, The Magnificence Project, LLC, and VisionCom, Inc., is a nationally recognized expert in the field of human potential. An award-winning author, speaker, transformational coach and mentor, Clardy has devoted her life to empowering individuals, organizations, and corporations to expand beyond perceived limitations into unlimited possibilities and true success.

A uniquely-gifted intuitive from birth, Clardy created The Prosperity Experiment, a life-changing workshop process, in 1998. The powerful process, now expanded into the Prosperity Academy's **Unlimited Energy Intensive**, cuts through the chaos of today's busy lifestyle to offer an innovative, joyful path to personal empowerment. The results can be astonishing. Her work has inspired thousands of people to move through limiting beliefs and behavior patterns to the triumph of true power.

Clardy holds an MFA from the Asolo Conservatory of Florida State University, an MA from the University of Missouri, and a BA cum laude from Beloit College. She studied in Europe at the Université de Haute Bretagne in Rennes, France, and at the Transpersonal Hypnotherapy Institute in Santa Monica, California. Clardy is also a graduate of the Hoffmann Quadrinity Process, and has studied with many notable human potential leaders.

Clardy currently serves as President of VisionCom, Inc. whose recent clients include Walt Disney Imagineering, Guthy-Renker, Inc., NBC Television, and Disney Cruise Line, among others. Prior to starting VisionCom, Clardy served as President and key developer of a multimillion dollar, bi-coastal entertainment corporation.

An avid environmentalist, Clardy received a nomination from The American Film Institute for her work on a TV/ video project entitled Save the Earth: A How-To Video. The program has been seen by millions of viewers across the world and has helped foster environmental awareness in schools throughout the United States and Canada. Clardy's work has been featured in many publications such as The

Los Angeles Times, USA Today, and on Entertainment Tonight and MTV.

A former resident of New York, Los Angeles, and Miami, Clardy now divides her time between New Smyrna Beach and Winter Park, Florida, where she lives with her two sons.

Anette